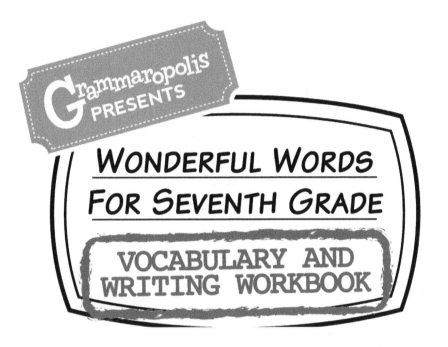

Grammaropolis PRESENTS

WONDERFUL WORDS
FOR SEVENTH GRADE

VOCABULARY AND WRITING WORKBOOK

BY ORDER OF

The Mayor of Grammaropolis

Written by Christopher Knight
Interior Design by Christopher Knight
Cover Design by Mckee Frazior
Grammaropolis Character Design by Powerhouse Animation & Mckee Frazior

ISBN: 9781644420577
Copyright © 2021 by Grammaropolis LLC
All rights reserved.
Published by Six Foot Press
Printed in the U.S.A.

Grammaropolis.com
SixFootPress.com

Grammaropolis
PRESENTS

WONDERFUL WORDS
FOR SEVENTH GRADE

VOCABULARY AND
WRITING WORKBOOK

GRAMMAROPOLIS BOOKS

HOUSTON

FROM THE DESK OF THE MAYOR

Greetings, fellow wordsmith!

Thank you so much for using this workbook. I hope you have fun learning some new vocabulary words!

As you know, many words can act as multiple parts of speech; it all depends on how they're used in the sentence. For the sake of clarity and simplicity (and because we didn't have enough space on the page!), the definitions in this workbook include only one part of speech for each word.

It's great to know a lot of vocabulary words, but the real reason we expand our vocabulary is so that we can communicate more effectively. That's why I've added a writing exercise, with optional prompts, at the end of each section.

Thanks again for visiting Grammaropolis. I hope you enjoy your stay!

—The Mayor

TABLE OF CONTENTS

How to Use the Vocabulary Pages

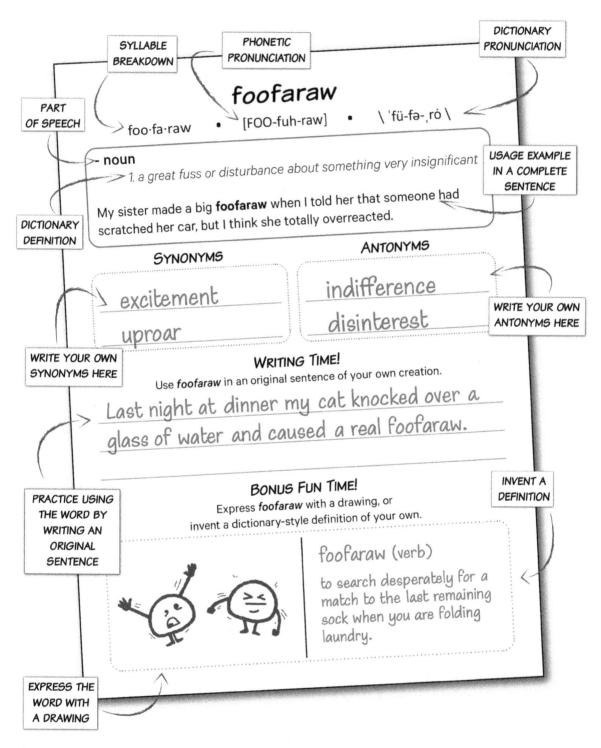

SYLLABLE BREAKDOWN

PHONETIC PRONUNCIATION

DICTIONARY PRONUNCIATION

foofaraw

PART OF SPEECH

foo·fa·raw • [FOO-fuh-raw] • \ ˈfü-fə-ˌrȯ \

noun

1. a great fuss or disturbance about something very insignificant

USAGE EXAMPLE IN A COMPLETE SENTENCE

My sister made a big **foofaraw** when I told her that someone had scratched her car, but I think she totally overreacted.

DICTIONARY DEFINITION

SYNONYMS

excitement

uproar

ANTONYMS

indifference

disinterest

WRITE YOUR OWN ANTONYMS HERE

WRITE YOUR OWN SYNONYMS HERE

WRITING TIME!
Use *foofaraw* in an original sentence of your own creation.

Last night at dinner my cat knocked over a glass of water and caused a real foofaraw.

PRACTICE USING THE WORD BY WRITING AN ORIGINAL SENTENCE

BONUS FUN TIME!
Express *foofaraw* with a drawing, or invent a dictionary-style definition of your own.

INVENT A DEFINITION

foofaraw (verb)

to search desperately for a match to the last remaining sock when you are folding laundry.

EXPRESS THE WORD WITH A DRAWING

Important Note: Synonyms and antonyms for nouns might be harder to come up with than they are for verbs and adjectives, but do your best!

THE PARTS OF SPEECH REVIEW

Every word acts as at least one of the eight parts of speech. In this workbook, you'll find nouns, verbs, and adjectives. Here are some things you need to remember about them!

NOUNS
A noun can name a person, place, thing, or idea.

<u>Naming a person:</u>
Jason is my very best **friend**.

<u>Naming a place:</u>
Becks Prime is my favorite **restaurant**.

<u>Naming a thing:</u>
That **ball** is my favorite **toy**.

<u>Naming an idea:</u>
Honesty and **loyalty** are my best **qualities**.

VERBS
An action verb expresses mental or physical action, and a linking verb expresses a state of being.

<u>Expressing physical action:</u>
Richard **jumped** across the river.

<u>Expressing mental action:</u>
Richard **considered** jumping across the river.

<u>Expressing a state of being:</u>
Richard **feels** bad. He **is** sorry for jumping across the river.

ADJECTIVES
*An adjective modifies a noun or a pronoun and tells **what kind, which one, how much,** or **how many.***

<u>Modifying a noun:</u>
The **quick brown** fox jumped over the **enormous red** fence at the **first** sign of trouble.

<u>Modifying a pronoun:</u>
They are **satisfied** with the answer, but I am still **curious**.

There are five other parts of speech you won't find in this workbook, but that doesn't mean they're not important!

ADVERBS
*An adverb modifies a verb, an adjective, or another adverb and tells **how, where, when,** or **to what extent.***

PRONOUNS
A pronoun takes the place of one or more nouns or pronouns.

PREPOSITIONS
A preposition shows a logical relationship or locates an object in time or space.

CONJUNCTIONS
A conjunction joins words or word groups.

INTERJECTIONS
An interjection expresses strong or mild emotion.

Wonderful Words for Seventh Grade Vocabulary & Writing Workbook ©2021 Grammaropolis LLC

SECTION ONE: WORD PREVIEW
Welcome to your ten new favorite words!

When you encounter a new word, take a moment to consider what it might mean.

1. Think about the word and circle what part of speech you think it is.
   *(Many words can act as more than one part of speech, depending on how they're used in the sentence, **so only choose one part of speech below**.)*
2. Come up with a brief definition of the word in the part of speech you've chosen. It doesn't have to be the *correct* definition—just do your best.

bewilder
Part of Speech: noun verb adjective

Definition:_____

_____

prediction
Part of Speech: noun verb adjective

Definition:_____

_____

emphasize
Part of Speech: noun verb adjective

Definition:_____

_____

connotation
Part of Speech: noun verb adjective

Definition:_____

_____

necessity
Part of Speech: noun verb adjective

Definition:_____

_____

component
Part of Speech: noun verb adjective

Definition:_____

_____

deceitful
Part of Speech: noun verb adjective

Definition:_____

_____

oppression
Part of Speech: noun verb adjective

Definition:_____

_____

consecutive
Part of Speech: noun verb adjective

Definition:_____

_____

punctual
Part of Speech: noun verb adjective

Definition:_____

_____

bewilder

be·wil·der   •   [bi-wIl-duhr]   •   \ bəˈwildər \

> **- verb**
>
> *1. to cause (someone) to become perplexed and confused*
>
> Dayton's explanation of how the vase broke **bewildered** his mother because it made no sense at all.

SYNONYMS

_____

_____

_____

ANTONYMS

_____

_____

_____

WRITING TIME!

Use *bewilder* in an original sentence of your own creation.

_____

_____

_____

BONUS FUN TIME!

Express *bewilder* with a drawing, or
invent a dictionary-style definition of your own.

prediction

pre·dic·tion   •   [pri-dIk-shuhn]   •   \ prəˈdikSH(ə)n \

- noun
> 1. a thing predicted : a forecast;
> 2. the action of predicting something

Carl made a **prediction** that nobody would turn in their paper in time, and he turned out to be right!

SYNONYMS

ANTONYMS

WRITING TIME!
Use *prediction* in an original sentence of your own creation.

BONUS FUN TIME!
Express *prediction* with a drawing, or
invent a dictionary-style definition of your own.

emphasize

em·pha·size   •   [Em-fuh-siez]   •   \ ˈemfəˌsīz \

- verb

   1. to give special importance or prominence to (something) in speaking or writing

The park ranger **emphasized** the importance of keeping food out of the tent so that bears wouldn't bother us.

SYNONYMS

ANTONYMS

WRITING TIME!

Use *emphasize* in an original sentence of your own creation.

BONUS FUN TIME!

Express *emphasize* with a drawing, or
invent a dictionary-style definition of your own.

connotation

con·no·ta·tion • [kahn-uh-tAY-shuhn] • \ ˌkänəˈtāSH(ə)n \

> **- noun**
>
> *1. an idea or feeling that a word invokes in addition to its literal or primary meaning*
>
> I don't know why the word "homework" has a negative **connotation** when it's really just work that you have to do at home. Oh, I get it now.

Synonyms

Antonyms

Writing Time!
Use *connotation* in an original sentence of your own creation.

Bonus Fun Time!
Express *connotation* with a drawing, or
invent a dictionary-style definition of your own.

necessity

ne·ces·si·ty • [ni-sEs-uh-tee] • \ nəˈsesədē \

- noun

1. the fact of being required or indispensable;

2. an indispensable thing

Lexi thinks that chocolate isn't very important, but it's a **necessity** for me!

SYNONYMS

ANTONYMS

WRITING TIME!

Use *necessity* in an original sentence of your own creation.

BONUS FUN TIME!

Express *necessity* with a drawing, or
invent a dictionary-style definition of your own.

component

com·po·nent • [kuhm-pOH-nuhnt] • \ kəmˈpōnənt \

- noun

1. *a part or element of a larger whole, especially a part of a machine or vehicle*

You need a magnifying glass if you want to repair a pocketwatch because the **components** inside are all so tiny.

SYNONYMS

ANTONYMS

WRITING TIME!

Use *component* in an original sentence of your own creation.

BONUS FUN TIME!

Express *component* with a drawing, or
invent a dictionary-style definition of your own.

deceitful

de·ceit·ful   •   [di-sEEt-fuhl]   •   \ dəˈsētfəl \

> **- adjective**
>
> *1. guilty of or involving deceit : deceiving or misleading others*
>
> It turns out that Donielle was being **deceitful** when she told me that her unicorn Beanie Baby was valuable; it's worth almost nothing!

SYNONYMS

_____
_____
_____

ANTONYMS

_____
_____
_____

WRITING TIME!
Use *deceitful* in an original sentence of your own creation.

_____

_____

BONUS FUN TIME!
Express *deceitful* with a drawing, or
invent a dictionary-style definition of your own.

oppression

op·pres·sion • [uh-prEsh-hun] • \ əˈpreSHən \

- **noun**

   1. prolonged cruel or unjust treatment or control;
   2. the state of being subject to unjust treatment or control

Too many members of our society have dealt with **oppression** and unfairness for far too long, so let's do something about that.

SYNONYMS

ANTONYMS

WRITING TIME!
Use *oppression* in an original sentence of your own creation.

BONUS FUN TIME!
Express *oppression* with a drawing, or
invent a dictionary-style definition of your own.

consecutive

con·sec·u·tive   •   [kuhn-sEk-yuh-tiv]   •   \ kənˈsekyədiv \

- adjective

1. following continuously in unbroken or logical sequence

We had to eat macaroni for three **consecutive** dinners because we cooked so much of it.

SYNONYMS

_____

_____

_____

ANTONYMS

_____

_____

_____

WRITING TIME!

Use *consecutive* in an original sentence of your own creation.

_____

_____

_____

BONUS FUN TIME!

Express *consecutive* with a drawing, or
invent a dictionary-style definition of your own.

punctual

punc·tu·al • [pUHngkchUH-wuhl] • \ ˈpəNG(k)(t)SH(o͞o)əl \

- adjective

1. happening or doing something at the agreed or proper time;
2. on time

Hank is always late, and that makes his extremely **punctual** girlfriend so annoyed with him.

SYNONYMS

ANTONYMS

WRITING TIME!

Use *punctual* in an original sentence of your own creation.

BONUS FUN TIME!

Express *punctual* with a drawing, or
invent a dictionary-style definition of your own.

SECTION ONE: WORD REVIEW

Congratulations on learning ten amazing new words! Remember that the whole point of learning new vocabulary is actually to use it, so let's put your new vocabulary to use.

1. Review the words you've learned. Consider what ideas come to mind when you say the words. How about when you read the definitions?
2. Circle at least **two** of your favorites. You'll get to use these when you write your very own story!

bewilder ——— verb
1. to cause (someone) to become perplexed and confused

prediction ——— noun
1. a thing predicted : a forecast;
2. the action of predicting something

emphasize ——— verb
1. to give special importance or prominence to (something) in speaking or writing

connotation ——— noun
1. an idea or feeling that a word invokes in addition to its literal or primary meaning

necessity ——— noun
1. the fact of being required or indispensable;
2. an indispensable thing

component ——— noun
1. a part or element of a larger whole, especially a part of a machine or vehicle

deceitful ——— adjective
1. guilty of or involving deceit : deceiving or misleading others

oppression ——— noun
1. prolonged cruel or unjust treatment or control;
2. the state of being subject to unjust treatment or control

consecutive ——— adjective
1. following continuously in unbroken or logical sequence

punctual ——— adjective
1. happening or doing something at the agreed or proper time;
2. on time

STORY ONE

1. List the words you've chosen:

_____

2. Write a story that incorporates all of your chosen words. If you can't think of anything to write about, consider these suggestions:
   - **Write a story that takes place at the circus.**
   - **Write a story in which your main character has just woken up from a coma.**

Title: _____

_____

_____

_____

_____

_____

_____

_____

_____

SECTION TWO: WORD PREVIEW
Welcome to your ten new favorite words!

When you encounter a new word, take a moment to consider what it might mean.

1. Think about the word and circle what part of speech you think it is.
   *(Many words can act as more than one part of speech, depending on how they're used in the sentence, **so only choose one part of speech below.**)*
2. Come up with a brief definition of the word in the part of speech you've chosen. It doesn't have to be the *correct* definition—just do your best.

antagonize
Part of Speech: noun   verb   adjective

Definition:_____

_____

attribute
Part of Speech: noun   verb   adjective

Definition:_____

_____

liaison
Part of Speech: noun   verb   adjective

Definition:_____

_____

industrious
Part of Speech: noun   verb   adjective

Definition:_____

_____

negligent
Part of Speech: noun   verb   adjective

Definition:_____

_____

acknowledge
Part of Speech: noun   verb   adjective

Definition:_____

_____

characterize
Part of Speech: noun   verb   adjective

Definition:_____

_____

evaluate
Part of Speech: noun   verb   adjective

Definition:_____

_____

agitate
Part of Speech: noun   verb   adjective

Definition:_____

_____

tentative
Part of Speech: noun   verb   adjective

Definition:_____

_____

antagonize

an·tag·o·nize • [an-tAgUH-niez] • \ anˈtagəˌnīz \

> **- verb**
>
> *1. to cause (someone) to become hostile*
>
> Don't **antagonize** your little sister, or she she will get angry and pull your hair.

SYNONYMS

ANTONYMS

WRITING TIME!
Use *antagonize* in an original sentence of your own creation.

BONUS FUN TIME!
Express *antagonize* with a drawing, or
invent a dictionary-style definition of your own.

attribute

at·trib·ute   •   [uh-trI-byoot]   •   \ ˈatrə͟byo͞ot \

> **- noun**
>
>   1. *a quality or feature regarded as a characteristic or inherent part of someone or something*
>
> Kevin's best **attribute** is his kindness toward strangers.

SYNONYMS

ANTONYMS

WRITING TIME!

Use *attribute* in an original sentence of your own creation.

_____

_____

_____

BONUS FUN TIME!

Express *attribute* with a drawing, or
invent a dictionary-style definition of your own.

liaison

li·ai·son • [IEE-uh-zahn] • \ ˈlēəˌzän \

- **noun**

> *1. a person who acts as a link to assist communication or cooperation between groups of people*

When we traveled to China, we had to find a **liaison** to help coordinate our activities with the other groups.

SYNONYMS

ANTONYMS

WRITING TIME!

Use *liaison* in an original sentence of your own creation.

BONUS FUN TIME!

Express *liaison* with a drawing, or
invent a dictionary-style definition of your own.

industrious

in·dus·tri·ous • [in-dUH-stree-uhs] • \ inˈdəstrēəs \

- adjective

1. diligent and hard-working

People say that ants are the most **industrious** of all invertebrate insects because they're always working.

SYNONYMS

ANTONYMS

WRITING TIME!
Use *industrious* in an original sentence of your own creation.

BONUS FUN TIME!
Express *industrious* with a drawing, or
invent a dictionary-style definition of your own.

negligent

neg·li·gent   •   [nE-gli-juhnt]   •   \ ˈnegləjənt \

- adjective

1. failing to take proper care in doing something

Gavin was supposed to take the cookies out of the oven on time, but he was **negligent** and forgot, so the cookies all burned.

SYNONYMS

ANTONYMS

WRITING TIME!
Use *negligent* in an original sentence of your own creation.

BONUS FUN TIME!
Express *negligent* with a drawing, or
invent a dictionary-style definition of your own.

acknowledge

ac·knowl·edge   •   [ik-nAHl-ij]   •   \ əkˈnäləj \

- verb

1. to accept or admit the existence or truth of;

2. to gesture that one has noticed or recognized (someone)

For some reason, some people still won't **acknowledge** that UFOs and aliens are real.

SYNONYMS

ANTONYMS

WRITING TIME!

Use *acknowledge* in an original sentence of your own creation.

BONUS FUN TIME!

Express *acknowledge* with a drawing, or
invent a dictionary-style definition of your own.

characterize

char·ac·ter·ize • [kAIR-ik-tuhr-riez] • \ ˈkerəktəˌrīz \

- verb

1. to describe the distinctive nature or features of

I would **characterize** my little sister as having a great sense of humor and an even greater ability to get mad about the littlest things.

SYNONYMS

ANTONYMS

WRITING TIME!
Use *characterize* in an original sentence of your own creation.

BONUS FUN TIME!
Express *characterize* with a drawing, or
invent a dictionary-style definition of your own.

evaluate

e·val·u·ate • [i-vAl-yuh-wayt] • \ əˈvalyəˌwāt \

> **- verb**
>
> *1. to form an idea of the amount, number, or value of : assess*
>
> The coach **evaluated** her potential players by making them do drills and sprints.

SYNONYMS

ANTONYMS

WRITING TIME!
Use *evaluate* in an original sentence of your own creation.

BONUS FUN TIME!
Express *evaluate* with a drawing, or
invent a dictionary-style definition of your own.

agitate

ag·i·tate   •   [Aj-uh-tayt]   •   \ ˈajəˌtāt \

- verb

    1. to make (someone) troubled or nervous;

    2. to stir or disturb (something, especially a liquid) briskly

The strange way that kid is looking over here really **agitates** me!

SYNONYMS

_____

_____

ANTONYMS

_____

_____

WRITING TIME!

Use *agitate* in an original sentence of your own creation.

_____

_____

_____

BONUS FUN TIME!

Express *agitate* with a drawing, or
invent a dictionary-style definition of your own.

tentative

ten·ta·tive   •   [tEn-tuh-tiv]   •   \ ˈten(t)ədiv \

> **- adjective**
>> *1. not certain or fixed : provisional;*
>> *2. done without confidence : hesitant*
>
> The little girl took a **tentative** step into the candy store because she wasn't sure she was allowed to go inside.

SYNONYMS

ANTONYMS

WRITING TIME!
Use *tentative* in an original sentence of your own creation.

BONUS FUN TIME!
Express *tentative* with a drawing, or
invent a dictionary-style definition of your own.

Section Two: Word Review

Congratulations on learning ten amazing new words! Remember that the whole point of learning new vocabulary is actually to use it, so let's put your new vocabulary to use.

1. Review the words you've learned. Consider what ideas come to mind when you say the words. How about when you read the definitions?
2. Circle at least **two** of your favorites. You'll get to use these when you write your very own story!

antagonize —— verb

1. to cause (someone) to become hostile

attribute —— noun

1. a quality or feature regarded as a characteristic or inherent part of someone or something

liaison —— noun

1. a person who acts as a link to assist communication or cooperation between groups of people

industrious — adjective

1. diligent and hard-working

negligent —— adjective

1. failing to take proper care in doing something

acknowledge —— verb

1. to accept or admit the existence or truth of;
2. to gesture that one has noticed or recognized (someone)

characterize —— verb

1. to describe the distinctive nature or features of

evaluate —— verb

1. to form an idea of the amount, number, or value of : assess

agitate —— verb

1. to make (someone) troubled or nervous;
2. to stir or disturb (something, especially a liquid) briskly

tentative —— adjective

1. not certain or fixed : provisional;
2. done without confidence : hesitant

STORY TWO

1. List the words you've chosen:

_____

2. Write a story that incorporates all of your chosen words. If you can't think of anything to write about, consider these suggestions:
   - **Write a story that ends with a car crash.**
   - **Write a story about a time when you were the most disappointed you have ever been.**

Title: _____

_____

_____

_____

_____

_____

_____

_____

_____

_____

_____

_____

_____

_____

_____

Wonderful Words for Seventh Grade Vocabulary & Writing Workbook ©2021 Grammaropolis LLC

Wonderful Words for Seventh Grade Vocabulary & Writing Workbook ©2021 Grammaropolis LLC

SECTION THREE: WORD PREVIEW
Welcome to your ten new favorite words!

When you encounter a new word, take a moment to consider what it might mean.

1. Think about the word and circle what part of speech you think it is.
   (*Many words can act as more than one part of speech, depending on how they're used in the sentence, **so only choose one part of speech below.***)
2. Come up with a brief definition of the word in the part of speech you've chosen. It doesn't have to be the *correct* definition—just do your best.

inevitable
Part of Speech: noun   verb   adjective

Definition:_____

_____

dawdle
Part of Speech: noun   verb   adjective

Definition:_____

_____

infuriate
Part of Speech: noun   verb   adjective

Definition:_____

_____

indifferent
Part of Speech: noun   verb   adjective

Definition:_____

_____

persuasive
Part of Speech: noun   verb   adjective

Definition:_____

_____

boycott
Part of Speech: noun   verb   adjective

Definition:_____

_____

famished
Part of Speech: noun   verb   adjective

Definition:_____

_____

bias
Part of Speech: noun   verb   adjective

Definition:_____

_____

intimidate
Part of Speech: noun   verb   adjective

Definition:_____

_____

admonish
Part of Speech: noun   verb   adjective

Definition:_____

_____

inevitable

in·ev·i·ta·ble • [i-nEv-uh-tuh-buhl] • \ inˈevidəb(ə)l \

- adjective

1. certain to happen : unavoidable

When I broke my dad's favorite lamp, I knew that a punishment was **inevitable**, so I didn't even try to get out of it.

SYNONYMS

ANTONYMS

WRITING TIME!
Use *inevitable* in an original sentence of your own creation.

BONUS FUN TIME!
Express *inevitable* with a drawing, or
invent a dictionary-style definition of your own.

dawdle

daw·dle   •   [dAWd-l]   •   \ ˈdôdl \

- verb

1. to waste time;

2. to move slowly and idly

Ursula likes to get things done quickly, so she always hates getting paired with partners who **dawdle**.

SYNONYMS

ANTONYMS

WRITING TIME!

Use *dawdle* in an original sentence of your own creation.

BONUS FUN TIME!

Express *dawdle* with a drawing, or
invent a dictionary-style definition of your own.

infuriate

in·fu·ri·ate • [in-fyUR-ee-ayt] • \ inˈfyo͞orēˌāt \

- verb

1. to make (someone) extremely angry and impatient

People who throw their trash on the ground **infuriate** me!

SYNONYMS

ANTONYMS

WRITING TIME!
Use *infuriate* in an original sentence of your own creation.

BONUS FUN TIME!
Express *infuriate* with a drawing, or
invent a dictionary-style definition of your own.

indifferent

in·dif·fer·ent • [in-dIf-uhr-ruhnt] • \ inˈdif(ə)rənt \

- adjective

    1. having no particular interest or sympathy;

    2. neither good nor bad : mediocre

Zelda tried to get her parents to care about the video game she was playing, but they were **indifferent** to it.

SYNONYMS

ANTONYMS

WRITING TIME!

Use *indifferent* in an original sentence of your own creation.

BONUS FUN TIME!

Express *indifferent* with a drawing, or
invent a dictionary-style definition of your own.

persuasive

per·sua·sive • [puhr-swAY-siv] • \ pərˈswāsiv \

- adjective

1. *skilled at persuading someone to do or believe something through reasoning or the use of temptation*

Carlos was very **persuasive** when he tried to convince me to skip school with him, but somehow I resisted.

SYNONYMS

ANTONYMS

WRITING TIME!

Use *persuasive* in an original sentence of your own creation.

BONUS FUN TIME!

Express *persuasive* with a drawing, or
invent a dictionary-style definition of your own.

boycott

boy·cott   •   [bOI-kaht]   •   \ ˈboiˌkät \

- noun

1. a punitive ban that forbids relations with certain groups, cooperation with a policy, or the handling of goods

Customers staged a **boycott** of the sneaker company's products when they found out about the conditions in the factories.

SYNONYMS

ANTONYMS

WRITING TIME!
Use *boycott* in an original sentence of your own creation.

BONUS FUN TIME!
Express *boycott* with a drawing, or
invent a dictionary-style definition of your own.

famished

fam·ished   •   [fAm-isht]   •   \ ˈfamiSHt \

- adjective

1. extremely hungry

We hadn't eaten all day, so we were **famished** by the time we sat down for dinner.

SYNONYMS

_____

_____

_____

ANTONYMS

_____

_____

_____

WRITING TIME!

Use *famished* in an original sentence of your own creation.

_____

_____

_____

BONUS FUN TIME!

Express *famished* with a drawing, or
invent a dictionary-style definition of your own.

bias

bi·as   •   [bIE-uhs]   •   \ ˈbīəs \

- noun

1. prejudice in favor of or against one thing, person, or group compared with another, usually in a way considered to be unfair

I have a **bias** against people who like dark chocolate, so I hope you're not one of those people.

SYNONYMS

ANTONYMS

WRITING TIME!
Use *bias* in an original sentence of your own creation.

BONUS FUN TIME!
Express *bias* with a drawing, or
invent a dictionary-style definition of your own.

intimidate

in·tim·i·date • [in-tIm-uh-dayt] • \ inˈtiməˌdāt \

> **- verb**
>
> *1. to frighten or overawe (someone), especially in order to make them do what one wants*
>
> That big angry bully **intimidated** Daphne into letting him get on the swings before it was his turn.

SYNONYMS

ANTONYMS

WRITING TIME!
Use *intimidate* in an original sentence of your own creation.

BONUS FUN TIME!
Express *intimidate* with a drawing, or
invent a dictionary-style definition of your own.

admonish

ad·mon·ish • [ad-mAHn-ish] • \ ˌədˈmäniSH \

- verb

1. to warn or reprimand someone firmly

My teacher **admonished** me to turn in my homework on time for once.

SYNONYMS

ANTONYMS

WRITING TIME!

Use *admonish* in an original sentence of your own creation.

BONUS FUN TIME!

Express *admonish* with a drawing, or
invent a dictionary-style definition of your own.

Section Three: Word Review

Congratulations on learning ten amazing new words! Remember that the whole point of learning new vocabulary is actually to use it, so let's put your new vocabulary to use.

1. Review the words you've learned. Consider what ideas come to mind when you say the words. How about when you read the definitions?
2. Circle at least **two** of your favorites. You'll get to use these when you write your very own story!

inevitable —— adjective
1. certain to happen : unavoidable

dawdle —— verb
1. to waste time;
2. to move slowly and idly

infuriate —— verb
1. to make (someone) extremely angry and impatient

indifferent —— adjective
1. having no particular interest or sympathy;
2. neither good nor bad : mediocre

persuasive —— adjective
1. skilled at persuading someone to do or believe something through reasoning or the use of temptation

boycott —— noun
1. a punitive ban that forbids relations with certain groups, cooperation with a policy, or the handling of goods

famished —— adjective
1. extremely hungry

bias —— noun
1. prejudice in favor of or against one thing, person, or group compared with another, usually in a way considered to be unfair

intimidate —— verb
1. to frighten or overawe (someone), especially in order to make them do what one wants

admonish —— verb
1. to warn or reprimand someone firmly

STORY THREE

1. List the words you've chosen:

_____

2. Write a story that incorporates all of your chosen words. If you can't think of anything to write about, consider these suggestions:
   - **Write a story in which you suddenly appear in the middle of your favorite television show.**
   - **Write a story about a character who teaches archery.**

Title: _____

_____

_____

_____

_____

_____

_____

_____

_____

_____

_____

SECTION FOUR: WORD PREVIEW
Welcome to your ten new favorite words!

When you encounter a new word, take a moment to consider what it might mean.

1. Think about the word and circle what part of speech you think it is.
   *(Many words can act as more than one part of speech, depending on how they're used in the sentence, **so only choose one part of speech below**.)*
2. Come up with a brief definition of the word in the part of speech you've chosen. It doesn't have to be the *correct* definition—just do your best.

obnoxious
Part of Speech: noun verb adjective

Definition:_____

_____

initiate
Part of Speech: noun verb adjective

Definition:_____

_____

exuberant
Part of Speech: noun verb adjective

Definition:_____

_____

copious
Part of Speech: noun verb adjective

Definition:_____

_____

competent
Part of Speech: noun verb adjective

Definition:_____

_____

devious
Part of Speech: noun verb adjective

Definition:_____

_____

abrasive
Part of Speech: noun verb adjective

Definition:_____

_____

perceive
Part of Speech: noun verb adjective

Definition:_____

_____

allege
Part of Speech: noun verb adjective

Definition:_____

_____

ludicrous
Part of Speech: noun verb adjective

Definition:_____

_____

obnoxious

ob·nox·ious • [ahb-nAHk-shuhs] • \ əbˈnäkSHəs \

- adjective

1. extremely unpleasant

That **obnoxious** group of teenagers over there is yelling and laughing so loudly that I can't concentrate!

SYNONYMS

ANTONYMS

WRITING TIME!
Use *obnoxious* in an original sentence of your own creation.

BONUS FUN TIME!
Express *obnoxious* with a drawing, or
invent a dictionary-style definition of your own.

initiate

in·i·ti·ate • [i-nIsh-ee-ayt] • \ i'niSHē͵āt \

- **verb**
    1. *to cause (a process or action) to begin;*
    2. *to admit (someone) into a secret or obscure society or group*

Before you **initiate** the countdown, make sure that the rocket is filled with the proper amount of fuel.

SYNONYMS

ANTONYMS

WRITING TIME!

Use *initiate* in an original sentence of your own creation.

BONUS FUN TIME!

Express *initiate* with a drawing, or
invent a dictionary-style definition of your own.

exuberant

ex·u·ber·ant • [ig-zOO-buhr-ruhnt] • \ igˈzoob(ə)rənt \

- adjective

1. filled with or characterized by a lively energy and excitement

Natalia is so **exuberant** and filled with joy that it's hard not to have her excitement for life rub off on you.

SYNONYMS

ANTONYMS

WRITING TIME!
Use *exuberant* in an original sentence of your own creation.

BONUS FUN TIME!
Express *exuberant* with a drawing, or
invent a dictionary-style definition of your own.

copious

co·pi·ous   •   [kOH-pee-uhs]   •   \ ˈkōpēəs \

- adjective
1. abundant in supply or quantity

That school is notorious for assigning **copious** homework, even on the weekends!

SYNONYMS

ANTONYMS

WRITING TIME!
Use *copious* in an original sentence of your own creation.

BONUS FUN TIME!
Express *copious* with a drawing, or
invent a dictionary-style definition of your own.

competent

com·pe·tent • [kAHm-puh-tuhnt] • \ ˈkämpədənt \

- adjective

1. having the necessary ability, knowledge, or skill to do something successfully

Our previous coach didn't know what he was doing, so it's nice to have someone **competent** in charge for a change.

SYNONYMS

ANTONYMS

WRITING TIME!
Use *competent* in an original sentence of your own creation.

BONUS FUN TIME!
Express *competent* with a drawing, or
invent a dictionary-style definition of your own.

devious

de·vi·ous   •   [dEE-vee-uhs]   •   \ ˈdēvēəs \

- adjective

1. showing a skillful use of underhanded tactics to achieve goals

You have to be careful of my **devious** older brother because otherwise he will trick you.

SYNONYMS

ANTONYMS

WRITING TIME!

Use *devious* in an original sentence of your own creation.

BONUS FUN TIME!

Express *devious* with a drawing, or
invent a dictionary-style definition of your own.

abrasive

a·bra·sive   •   [uh-brAY-siv]   •   \ əˈbrāsiv \

- adjective

1. (of a substance or material) capable of polishing or cleaning a hard surface by rubbing or grinding

The more **abrasive** the sandpaper, the greater the effect it will have on the wood.

SYNONYMS

ANTONYMS

WRITING TIME!

Use *abrasive* in an original sentence of your own creation.

BONUS FUN TIME!

Express *abrasive* with a drawing, or
invent a dictionary-style definition of your own.

perceive

per·ceive   •   [puhr-sEEv]   •   \ pərˈsēv \

- verb
> *1. to become aware or conscious of (something);*
> *2. to interpret (something) in a particular way*

Carolyn **perceived** that her customers wanted more dinner options even though nobody actually told her that.

SYNONYMS

ANTONYMS

WRITING TIME!
Use *perceive* in an original sentence of your own creation.

BONUS FUN TIME!
Express *perceive* with a drawing, or
invent a dictionary-style definition of your own.

allege

al·lege   •   [uh-lEj]   •   \ əˈlej \

- adjective

> *1. to claim or assert that someone has done something illegal or wrong, typically without proof that this is the case.*

Carlton **alleged** that I had stolen his pudding at lunch, but he couldn't prove that it was me who did it.

SYNONYMS

ANTONYMS

WRITING TIME!
Use *allege* in an original sentence of your own creation.

BONUS FUN TIME!
Express *allege* with a drawing, or
invent a dictionary-style definition of your own.

ludicrous

lu·di·crous   •   [lOO-duh-kruhs]   •   \ ˈlo͞odəkrəs \

- adjective

1. so foolish, unreasonable, or out of place as to be amusing

Fabian's excuse for not turning in his homework was so **ludicrous** that Mr. Cordes laughed instead of getting mad.

SYNONYMS

_____

_____

_____

ANTONYMS

_____

_____

_____

WRITING TIME!
Use *ludicrous* in an original sentence of your own creation.

_____

_____

_____

BONUS FUN TIME!
Express *ludicrous* with a drawing, or
invent a dictionary-style definition of your own.

SECTION FOUR: WORD REVIEW

Congratulations on learning ten amazing new words! Remember that the whole point of learning new vocabulary is actually to use it, so let's put your new vocabulary to use.

1. Review the words you've learned. Consider what ideas come to mind when you say the words. How about when you read the definitions?
2. Circle at least **two** of your favorites. You'll get to use these when you write your very own story!

obnoxious — adjective
1. extremely unpleasant

initiate — verb
1. to cause (a process or action) to begin;
2. to admit (someone) into a secret or obscure society or group

exuberant — adjective
1. filled with or characterized by a lively energy and excitement

copious — adjective
1. abundant in supply or quantity

competent — adjective
1. having the necessary ability, knowledge, or skill to do something successfully

devious — adjective
1. showing a skillful use of underhanded tactics to achieve goals

abrasive — adjective
1. (of a substance or material) capable of polishing or cleaning a hard surface by rubbing or grinding

perceive — verb
1. to become aware or conscious of (something);
2. to interpret (something) in a particular way

allege — verb
1. to claim or assert that someone has done something illegal or wrong, typically without proof that this is the case.

ludicrous — adjective
1. so foolish, unreasonable, or out of place as to be amusing

STORY FOUR

1. List the words you've chosen:

_____

2. Write a story that incorporates all of your chosen words. If you can't think of anything to write about, consider these suggestions:
   - **Write a story that takes place in a dog park.**
   - **Write a story that takes place exactly one year from now.**

Title: _____

_____

_____

_____

_____

_____

_____

_____

_____

Wonderful Words for Seventh Grade Vocabulary & Writing Workbook ©2021 Grammaropolis LLC

SECTION FIVE: WORD PREVIEW
Welcome to your ten new favorite words!

When you encounter a new word, take a moment to consider what it might mean.

1. Think about the word and circle what part of speech you think it is.
*(Many words can act as more than one part of speech, depending on how they're used in the sentence, **so only choose one part of speech below.**)*

2. Come up with a brief definition of the word in the part of speech you've chosen. It doesn't have to be the *correct* definition—just do your best.

eligible
Part of Speech: noun verb adjective

*Definition:*_____

_____

sovereign
Part of Speech: noun verb adjective

*Definition:*_____

_____

talisman
Part of Speech: noun verb adjective

*Definition:*_____

_____

prospective
Part of Speech: noun verb adjective

*Definition:*_____

_____

condemn
Part of Speech: noun verb adjective

*Definition:*_____

_____

confront
Part of Speech: noun verb adjective

*Definition:*_____

_____

derogatory
Part of Speech: noun verb adjective

*Definition:*_____

_____

prominent
Part of Speech: noun verb adjective

*Definition:*_____

_____

inhabitant
Part of Speech: noun verb adjective

*Definition:*_____

_____

abdicate
Part of Speech: noun verb adjective

*Definition:*_____

_____

eligible

el·i·gi·ble • [El-uh-juh-buhl] • \ ˈeləjəb(ə)l \

> **- adjective**
> 1. *having the right to do or obtain something;*
> 2. *satisfying the appropriate conditions*
>
> Henry couldn't enter the contest because only people from New Mexico were **eligible**, and Henry is from Colorado.

Synonyms

Antonyms

Writing Time!
Use *eligible* in an original sentence of your own creation.

Bonus Fun Time!
Express *eligible* with a drawing, or
invent a dictionary-style definition of your own.

sovereign

sov·er·eign • [sAHv-ruhn] • \ ˈsäv(ə)rən \

- adjective

1. possessing supreme or ultimate power;

2. acting or done independently and without outside interference

Mrs. Jenkins told us that she is the **sovereign** leader of her classroom, so we're not allowed to tell her what to do.

SYNONYMS

ANTONYMS

WRITING TIME!

Use *sovereign* in an original sentence of your own creation.

BONUS FUN TIME!

Express *sovereign* with a drawing, or
invent a dictionary-style definition of your own.

talisman

tal·is·man • [tAl-uh-smuhn] • \ ˈtaləsmən \

- noun

> *1. an object, typically an inscribed ring or stone, that is thought to have magic powers and to bring good luck*

Things have been going well for me ever since I crafted a **talisman** out of a smooth rock I found in the forest.

SYNONYMS

ANTONYMS

WRITING TIME!

Use *talisman* in an original sentence of your own creation.

BONUS FUN TIME!

Express *talisman* with a drawing, or
invent a dictionary-style definition of your own.

prospective

pro·spec·tive • [pruh-spEk-tiv] • \ prəˈspektiv \

- **adjective**
  1. *likely to happen at a future date;*
  2. *concerned with or applying to the future*

The **prospective** students toured their new school to get a sense of what the classes would be like.

SYNONYMS

ANTONYMS

WRITING TIME!
Use *prospective* in an original sentence of your own creation.

BONUS FUN TIME!
Express *prospective* with a drawing, or
invent a dictionary-style definition of your own.

condemn

con·demn • [kuhn-dEm] • \ kənˈdem \

- verb
> 1. *to express complete disapproval of, typically in public;*
> 2. *to sentence (someone) to a punishment, especially death*

It's not enough simply to mention that we don't allow racism; we must strongly **condemn** racism with our words and actions.

SYNONYMS

ANTONYMS

WRITING TIME!
Use *condemn* in an original sentence of your own creation.

BONUS FUN TIME!
Express *condemn* with a drawing, or
invent a dictionary-style definition of your own.

confront

con·front • [kuhn-frUHnt] • \ kənˈfrənt \

- verb

1. to meet face to face with hostile or argumentative intent;

2. face up to and deal with (a problem or difficult situation)

Hector **confronted** his friend about the missing cheesecake, but I was too afraid to say anything.

SYNONYMS

ANTONYMS

WRITING TIME!

Use *confront* in an original sentence of your own creation.

BONUS FUN TIME!

Express *confront* with a drawing, or
invent a dictionary-style definition of your own.

derogatory

de·rog·a·to·ry • [di-rAHgUH-tor-ee] • \ dəˈrägəˌtôrē \

- adjective

1. showing a critical or disrespectful attitude

Saying **derogatory** things about someone is likely to make that person upset.

SYNONYMS	ANTONYMS

WRITING TIME!

Use *derogatory* in an original sentence of your own creation.

BONUS FUN TIME!

Express *derogatory* with a drawing, or
invent a dictionary-style definition of your own.

prominent

prom·i·nent • [prAHm-uh-nuhnt] • \ ˈprämənənt \

- adjective

   1. important : famous;

   2. situated so as to catch the attention : noticeable

The Mayor is one of the most **prominent** citizens in the whole city of Grammaropolis.

SYNONYMS

ANTONYMS

WRITING TIME!

Use *prominent* in an original sentence of your own creation.

BONUS FUN TIME!

Express *prominent* with a drawing, or
invent a dictionary-style definition of your own.

inhabitant

in·hab·it·ant • [in-hAb-uh-tuhnt] • \ inˈhabədnt \

- noun

1. a person or animal that lives in or occupies a certain place

Some of the **inhabitants** of my hometown miss me, but not everyone who lives there was sad to see me leave!

SYNONYMS

ANTONYMS

WRITING TIME!
Use *inhabitant* in an original sentence of your own creation.

BONUS FUN TIME!
Express *inhabitant* with a drawing, or
invent a dictionary-style definition of your own.

abdicate

ab·di·cate • [Ab-di-kayt] • \ ˈabdəˌkāt \

- verb

1. to fail to fulfill or undertake (a responsibility or duty);

2. of a monarch) to renounce one's throne

Kelso was supposed to be our leader, but he **abdicated** his role, so we had nobody to tell us what we needed to do.

SYNONYMS

ANTONYMS

WRITING TIME!

Use *abdicate* in an original sentence of your own creation.

BONUS FUN TIME!

Express *abdicate* with a drawing, or
invent a dictionary-style definition of your own.

SECTION FIVE: WORD REVIEW

Congratulations on learning ten amazing new words! Remember that the whole point of learning new vocabulary is actually to use it, so let's put your new vocabulary to use.

1. Review the words you've learned. Consider what ideas come to mind when you say the words. How about when you read the definitions?
2. Circle at least **two** of your favorites. You'll get to use these when you write your very own story!

eligible —— adjective
1. having the right to do or obtain something;
2. satisfying the appropriate conditions

sovereign —— adjective
1. possessing supreme or ultimate power;
2. acting or done independently and without outside interference

talisman —— noun
1. an object, typically an inscribed ring or stone, that is thought to have magic powers and to bring good luck

prospective —— adjective
1. likely to happen at a future date;
2. concerned with or applying to the future

condemn —— verb
1. to express complete disapproval of, typically in public;
2. to sentence (someone) to a punishment, especially death

confront —— verb
1. to meet face to face with hostile or argumentative intent;
2. face up to and deal with (a problem or difficult situation)

derogatory —— adjective
1. showing a critical or disrespectful attitude

prominent —— adjective
1. important : famous;
2. situated so as to catch the attention : noticeable

inhabitant —— noun
1. a person or animal that lives in or occupies a certain place

abdicate —— verb
1. to fail to fulfill or undertake (a responsibility or duty);
2. of a monarch) to renounce one's throne

STORY FIVE

1. List the words you've chosen:

_____

2. Write a story that incorporates all of your chosen words. If you can't think of anything to write about, consider these suggestions:
   - **Write a story that includes knights, dragons, sheep, and candy corn.**
   - **Write a story inspired by your earliest memory.**

Title: _____

_____

_____

_____

_____

_____

_____

_____

_____

_____

_____

_____

_____

_____

Wonderful Words for Seventh Grade Vocabulary & Writing Workbook ©2021 Grammaropolis LLC

SECTION SIX: WORD PREVIEW
Welcome to your ten new favorite words!

When you encounter a new word, take a moment to consider what it might mean.

1. Think about the word and circle what part of speech you think it is.
   (Many words can act as more than one part of speech, depending on how they're used in the sentence, **so only choose one part of speech below.**)
2. Come up with a brief definition of the word in the part of speech you've chosen. It doesn't have to be the *correct* definition—just do your best.

authentic
Part of Speech: noun   verb   adjective

Definition:_____

_____

irate
Part of Speech: noun   verb   adjective

Definition:_____

_____

mitigate
Part of Speech: noun   verb   adjective

Definition:_____

_____

bamboozle
Part of Speech: noun   verb   adjective

Definition:_____

_____

treason
Part of Speech: noun   verb   adjective

Definition:_____

_____

naive
Part of Speech: noun   verb   adjective

Definition:_____

_____

formidable
Part of Speech: noun   verb   adjective

Definition:_____

_____

libel
Part of Speech: noun   verb   adjective

Definition:_____

_____

candor
Part of Speech: noun   verb   adjective

Definition:_____

_____

demeanor
Part of Speech: noun   verb   adjective

Definition:_____

_____

authentic

au·then·tic   •   [uh-thEn-tik]   •   \ ô'THen(t)ik \

> **- adjective**
>   1. *of undisputed origin : genuine;*
>   2. *based on facts : accurate or reliable*
>
> Is that an **authentic** baseball card, or did someone make a fake one?

SYNONYMS

ANTONYMS

WRITING TIME!
Use *authentic* in an original sentence of your own creation.

BONUS FUN TIME!
Express *authentic* with a drawing, or
invent a dictionary-style definition of your own.

irate

i·rate   •   [ie-rAYt]   •   \ ī'rāt \

- adjective

1. feeling or characterized by great anger

The restaurant manager became **irate** when a group of young rapscallions tried to leave without paying for their meal.

SYNONYMS

ANTONYMS

WRITING TIME!

Use *irate* in an original sentence of your own creation.

BONUS FUN TIME!

Express *irate* with a drawing, or
invent a dictionary-style definition of your own.

mitigate

mit·i·gate • [mlt-uh-gayt] • \ ˈmidəˌgāt \

- verb

1. to make less severe, serious, or painful

Putting on sunscreen will **mitigate** the negative effect of the sun's UV rays on your skin.

SYNONYMS

ANTONYMS

WRITING TIME!
Use *mitigate* in an original sentence of your own creation.

BONUS FUN TIME!
Express *mitigate* with a drawing, or
invent a dictionary-style definition of your own.

bamboozle

bam·boo·zle • [bam-bOO-zuhl] • \ bam'boozəl \

- verb

    1. to fool or cheat (someone);

    2. to confound or perplex

I can usually tell when I am being conned, but that guy on the corner totally **bamboozled** me with his card trick.

SYNONYMS

ANTONYMS

WRITING TIME!

Use *bamboozle* in an original sentence of your own creation.

BONUS FUN TIME!

Express *bamboozle* with a drawing, or
invent a dictionary-style definition of your own.

treason

trea·son   •   [trEEz-n]   •   \ ˈtrēzən \

- noun

1. the action or crime of betraying someone or something

When Sasha telling the other team our exact strategy was a **treason** against the people who were counting on her!

SYNONYMS

ANTONYMS

WRITING TIME!
Use *treason* in an original sentence of your own creation.

BONUS FUN TIME!
Express *treason* with a drawing, or
invent a dictionary-style definition of your own.

naive

na·ive • [nah-EEv] • \ nīˈēv \

- adjective

1. showing a lack of experience, wisdom, or judgment;

2. (of a person) natural and unaffected

I should have known that my opponent would cheat, but I was **naive** and figured that he would play by the rules.

Synonyms

Antonyms

Writing Time!

Use *naive* in an original sentence of your own creation.

Bonus Fun Time!

Express *naive* with a drawing, or
invent a dictionary-style definition of your own.

formidable

for·mi·da·ble • [fOR-muh-duh-buhl] • \ ˈfôrmədəb(ə)l \

- adjective

1. inspiring fear or respect through being impressively large, powerful, intense, or capable

The Mountaineers are our most **formidable** opponent yet because they haven't lost a game all season.

SYNONYMS

ANTONYMS

WRITING TIME!

Use *formidable* in an original sentence of your own creation.

BONUS FUN TIME!

Express *formidable* with a drawing, or
invent a dictionary-style definition of your own.

libel

li·bel   •   [lIE-buhl]   •   \ ˈlībəl \

- noun

1. the action or crime of publishing a false statement about a person

Our local newspaper got in trouble for **libel** because it printed something disparaging about the Mayor that everyone knew was false.

SYNONYMS

ANTONYMS

WRITING TIME!

Use *libel* in an original sentence of your own creation.

BONUS FUN TIME!

Express *libel* with a drawing, or
invent a dictionary-style definition of your own.

candor

can·dor   •   [kAHn-dor]   •   \ ˈkandər \

- noun

    1. the quality of being open and honest in expression : frankness

I always appreciate Rudy's **candor** even though sometimes her honesty makes me uncomfortable.

SYNONYMS

ANTONYMS

WRITING TIME!
Use *candor* in an original sentence of your own creation.

BONUS FUN TIME!
Express *candor* with a drawing, or
invent a dictionary-style definition of your own.

demeanor

de·mean·or • [di-mEE-nuhr] • \ dəˈmēnər \

- noun

1. outward behavior or bearing

Julian projected a calm and confident **demeanor**, but he was actually terrified inside.

SYNONYMS

ANTONYMS

WRITING TIME!

Use *demeanor* in an original sentence of your own creation.

BONUS FUN TIME!

Express *demeanor* with a drawing, or
invent a dictionary-style definition of your own.

Section Six: Word Review

Congratulations on learning ten amazing new words! Remember that the whole point of learning new vocabulary is actually to use it, so let's put your new vocabulary to use.

1. Review the words you've learned. Consider what ideas come to mind when you say the words. How about when you read the definitions?
2. Circle at least *two* of your favorites. You'll get to use these when you write your very own story!

authentic —— adjective

1. of undisputed origin : genuine;
2. based on facts : accurate or reliable

irate —— adjective

1. feeling or characterized by great anger

mitigate —— verb

1. to make less severe, serious, or painful

bamboozle —— verb

1. to fool or cheat (someone);
2. to confound or perplex

treason —— noun

1. the action or crime of betraying someone or something

naive —— adjective

1. showing a lack of experience, wisdom, or judgment;
2. (of a person) natural and unaffected

formidable —— adjective

1. inspiring fear or respect through being impressively large, powerful, intense, or capable

libel —— noun

1. the action or crime of publishing a false statement about a person

candor —— noun

1. the quality of being open and honest in expression : frankness

demeanor —— noun

1. outward behavior or bearing

STORY SIX

1. List the words you've chosen:

_____

2. Write a story that incorporates all of your chosen words. If you can't think of anything to write about, consider these suggestions:
   - **Write a story that starts with you preparing your favorite dessert.**
   - **Write a story that takes place in a world where people ride giant Chihuahua dogs instead of driving around in cars.**

Title: _____

_____

_____

_____

_____

_____

_____

_____

_____

_____

_____

_____

_____

_____

Wonderful Words for Seventh Grade Vocabulary & Writing Workbook ©2021 Grammaropolis LLC

Wonderful Words for Seventh Grade Vocabulary & Writing Workbook ©2021 Grammaropolis LLC

INDEX OF WORDS USED

Printed in the USA
CPSIA information can be obtained
at www.ICGtesting.com
JSHW060042150824
68134JS00028B/2605